"Do not c
learning, fc

....

....

....

....

....

....

....

....

....

....

....

....

....

....

....

....

....

....

....

....

....

....

....

....

....

....

....

....

....

....

....

"If kids come to us from strong, healthy functioning families, it makes our job easier. If they do not come to us from strong, healthy, functioning families, it makes our job more important." (Barbara Colorose)

....

....

....

....

....

....

....

....

....

....

....

....

....

....

....

....

....

....

....

....

....

....

....

....

....

....

....

....

....

....

....

"What we want is to see the child in pursuit of knowledge, and not knowledge in pursuit of the child." (George Bernard Shaw)

"We're trying to give the young people something that can help them, and we don't know exactly what it ought to be."
(Wendell Berry)

"Teaching is the greatest act of optimism."
(Colleen Wilcox)

"Students don't care how much you know until they know how much you care." (Anonymous)

"The dream begins, most of the time, with a teacher who believes in you, who tugs and pushes and leads you on to the next plateau, sometimes poking you with a sharp stick called truth." (Dan Rather)

"Good teaching is one-fourth preparation and three-fourths theater." (Gail Goldwin)

"The art of teaching is the art of assisting discovery." (Mark Van Doren)

"Teaching is not a lost art, but the regard for it is a lost tradition." (Jacques Barzun)

"Education is not the filling of a pail, but the lighting of a fire." (William Butler Yeats)

"I'm not sayin' I'm gonna change the world, but I guarantee that I will spark the brain that will."
(Tupac Shakur)

"Education is not preparation for life; education is life itself." (John Dewey)

"I have come to believe that a great teacher is a great artist and that there are as few as there are any other great artists. It might even be the greatest of the arts since the medium is the human mind and spirit." (John Steinbeck)

"The mediocre teacher tells. The good teacher explains. The superior teacher demonstrates. The great teacher inspires." (William Ward)

"Everything should be made as simple as possible, but not simpler." (Einstein)

"We learn geology the morning after the earthquake." (Ralph Waldo Emerson)

"There is no failure. Only feedback."
(Robert Allen)

"The direction in which education starts a man will determine his future life." (Plato)

....

....

....

....

....

....

....

....

....

....

....

....

....

....

....

....

....

....

....

....

....

....

....

....

....

....

....

....

....

....

....

"If you are planning for a year, sow rice; if you are planning for a decade, plant trees; if you are planning for a lifetime, educate people."
(Chinese Proverb)

....

....

....

....

....

....

....

....

....

....

....

....

....

....

....

....

....

....

....

....

....

....

....

....

....

....

....

....

....

....

....

"Death is not the greatest loss. The greatest loss is what dies inside while still alive. Never surrender." (Tupac Shakur)

"A good teacher is like a candle – it consumes itself to light the way for others."
(Mustafa Kemal Atatürk)

"The more that you read, the more things you will know, the more that you learn, the more places you'll go." (Dr. Seuss)

....

....

....

....

....

....

....

....

....

....

....

....

....

....

....

....

....

....

....

....

....

....

....

....

....

....

....

....

....

....

....

"I am not a teacher, but an awakener."
(Robert Frost)

....
....
....
....
....
....
....
....
....
....
....
....
....
....
....
....
....
....
....
....
....
....
....
....
....
....
....
....
....
....
....

"It takes a big heart to help shape little minds."
(Unknown)

"Teaching kids to count is fine, but teaching them what counts is best." (Bob Talbert)

"You cannot teach a crab to walk straight."
(Aristophenes)

"If a child can't learn the way we teach, maybe we should teach the way they learn."
(Ignacio 'Nacho' Estrada)

....
....
....
....
....
....
....
....
....
....
....
....
....
....
....
....
....
....
....
....
....
....
....
....
....
....
....
....
....
....
....

"You are the bows from which your children as living arrows are sent forth." (Khalil Gibran)

....

....

....

....

....

....

....

....

....

....

....

....

....

....

....

....

....

....

....

....

....

....

....

....

....

....

....

....

....

....

....

"One looks back with appreciation to the brilliant teachers, but with gratitude to those who touched our human feelings. The curriculum is so much necessary raw material, but warmth is the vital element for the growing plant and for the soul of the child." (Carl Jung)

....
....
....
....
....
....
....
....
....
....
....
....
....
....
....
....
....
....
....
....
....
....
....
....
....
....
....
....
....
....
....

"Teaching is the one profession that creates all other professions." (Unknown)

"In a completely rational society, the best of us would be teachers and the rest of us would have to settle for something less." (Lee Iacocca)

"I cannot teach anybody anything, I can only make them think." (Socrates)

"Remember that failure is an event, not a person." (Zig Ziglar)

"It may be that when we no longer know which way to go that we have come to our real journey. The mind that is not baffled is not employed. The impeded stream is the one that sings."
(Wendell Berry)

"Learning is not a spectator sport." (D. Blocher)

"The next best thing to knowing something is knowing where to find it" (Samuel Johnson)

"Never discourage anyone…who continually makes progress, no matter how slow." (Plato)

"The eye sees only what the mind is prepared to comprehend." (Henri Bergson)

....

....

....

....

....

....

....

....

....

....

....

....

....

....

....

....

....

....

....

....

....

....

....

....

....

....

....

....

....

....

....

'I never teach my pupils. I only attempt to provide the conditions in which they can learn."
(Einstein)

"Education breeds confidence. Confidence breeds hope. Hope breeds peace." (Confucius)

....

....

....

....

....

....

....

....

....

....

....

....

....

....

....

....

....

....

....

....

....

....

....

....

....

....

....

....

....

....

....

"There is a great difference between knowing and understanding: you can know a lot about something and not really understand it."
(Charles F. Kettering)

....

....

....

....

....

....

....

....

....

....

....

....

....

....

....

....

....

....

....

....

....

....

....

....

....

....

....

....

....

....

....

"I like a teacher who gives you something to take home to think about besides homework."
(Lily Tomlin)

"What the teacher is, is more important than what he teaches." (Karl Meninger)

"Opportunity is missed by most people because it is dressed in overalls and looks like work."
(Thomas Edison)

"Thought flows in terms of stories–stories about events, stories about people, and stories about intentions and achievements. The best teachers are the best story tellers. We learn in the form of stories." (Frank Martin)

"You can't direct the wind but you can adjust the sails." (Anonymous)

....

....

....

....

....

....

....

....

....

....

....

....

....

....

....

....

....

....

....

....

....

....

....

....

....

....

....

....

....

....

....

"The best teachers teach from the heart, not from the book." (Unknown)

....
....
....
....
....
....
....
....
....
....
....
....
....
....
....
....
....
....
....
....
....
....
....
....
....
....
....
....
....
....
....

“Spoon feeding in the long run teaches us nothing but the shape of the spoon.”
(E. M. Forster)

"If we teach today's students as we taught yesterday's, we rob them of tomorrow."
(John Dewey)

73688831R00057

Made in the USA
Lexington, KY
11 December 2017